SHACKS, SHELTERS & SHANTY TOWNS

With the migration of workers from rural settlements to the cities across South Africa, informal communities have been established on undeveloped land in closer proximity to towns and cities.

Resourceful residents have created makeshift homes and like a brightly woven patchwork quilt, as the shacks cover the dusty landscape, the earth comes to life with a surreal and gritty beauty.

A colourful sub-culture has sprung up from the streets of the townships – complete with its own township slang, vibrant art and informal industries like the outdoor hairdresser, the pavement fruit-seller, and the corner 'spaza' shop, and a bustling taxi fleet ferries workers to and from their place of work. Regardless of their circumstances, residents display a hopefulness that this Rainbow Nation will evolve to meet their needs, and those of all her people.

Homes are precariously built with salvaged pieces of cardboard, wood, corrugated iron and chipboard. Generous splashes of colour uplift them from these tawdry foundations. Enterprising residents use whatever has been abandoned, traded or donated to improve and enhance. A sense of self-worth is ever-present as can be seen in the freshly-washed garments that hang out in the humble backyard.

Oil lamps, candles and torchlight illuminate the rooms in a gentle wash of magical light. For those who do not yet have electricity, as in days gone by, paraffin stoves will boil the kettle and candles will light the way.

Each room has its own décor of distinctive character and charm. Ingenious space saving methods are essential in the diminutive quarters.

Bicycles hang like massive mobiles above beds, beds become couches during the day.

There exists a strong sense of community amongst the shack dwellers, a generosity beyond means, a fellowship of pride. With no official demarcation of land, neighbours must share a courtyard and be prepared to offer up any spare space if a new home needs to be erected.

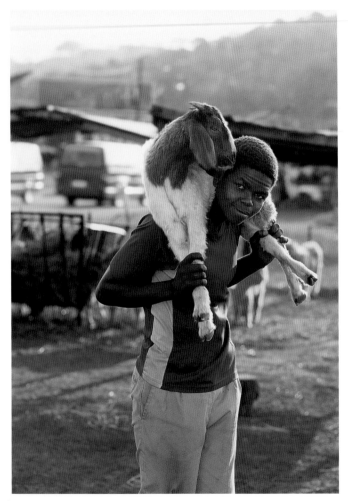

Vegetable patches and banana trees are carefully nurtured, usually by the women and children of the community as the men are often away at work. For those living on the breadline, these crops go a long way to feed their families.

14

The spirit in these humble surrounds is overwhelmingly joyous and welcoming. An exuberant throng of children eagerly awaits their turn on a round-a-bout in the village. Growing up with few material assets, it is more often the children's playful imaginations that will keep them occupied until their parents call them in for the evening meal.

An entrepreneurial temperament is ever burgeoning. An old beer crate and crudely cut chipboard become a makeshift table selling an assortment of sweets. A vintage sewing machine is the indispensable tool for a thriving sewing business.

Vivid hues of sunshine and sky beckon customers to the local spaza shop.   Enjoy a Coca-Cola, have a mug of sweet tea, sit, chat and relax.   Life is slow here, and away from the rat race of the cities, time beats to a mellow tune.

A vegetable shop of red, green and gold visually croons that laid-back reggae vibe. Bob Marley and Haile Selassi keep watch over the apples and bananas.

Individuality abounds in these settlements and never ceases to captivate the imagination.

Friendly faces and ubiquitous South African brands speak of familiarity and trust. Like many African communities, there is an allegiance to certain products that have been around for generations.

Braiding or shaving, salons in the sun are a familiar sight as locals keep abreast of the latest fashion trends. So sit down on an old beer crate and let the professionals make you look hip and happening!

Out here, even strangers are treated like family. Jovial voices holler greetings of a brand new and blessed day. Everywhere bright smiles echo the radiant sun. There exists a wonderful camaraderie that is sadly lost in exclusive suburbia.

A stockpile of second-hand bricks resting against a vividly coloured tin shack allude to the owner's dream of a solid brick house.

Kaleidoscopic houses paint a vibrant picture on the dunes. Each and every shack is spontaneously unique. An unequivocal sign that cultural creativity is evolving with the times. As more and more formal housing is being built however, these animated structures will almost surely be a page in the history books of South Africa.

Murals of allegiance to a favourite soccer team, etchings and graffiti all serve to individualise the exteriors of the homes. Soccer is the most popular sport amongst black South Africans. Kaizer Chiefs and Orlando Pirates are teams that both hail from Soweto, and when they play against each other it is one of the most fanatical and popular soccer derbys worldwide. A stadium that seats 80 000 has been known to be filled with 95 000 frenzied fans.

The soul of the shanty towns is often to be found in the local shebeens – popular bars playing music and selling beer, liquor and intoxicating home-brews. In the past shebeens helped to create a new working-class culture. They became the method of survival for musicians and shebeen queens (tavern owners) who could rely on this money instead of going off to work in an ominous mine or a factory. These days some can afford the luxury of a pool table, while others see customers playing dice or cards.

Unlike the indigenous housing of the past of mud, wattle, sticks or branches, these informal settlements use leftover wooden planks, advertising boards, cardboard, corrugated iron, plastic, tarpaulins and chipboard.

An overwhelming vivacity of spirit. A tangible feeling of pride. For all their undeniable poverty, the people have found a content disposition that money seldom buys, as these cheerful children with their ready smiles attest to.

A lightening streak of liquid yellow and orange rages through the sleepy shacks. Very few people have their own transport and therefore rely on the public trains and buses or the privately owned mini-bus taxis.

Flamboyant in colour as it is ebullient in sound. With an ever-thumping ethnic beat, the mini-bus taxis squeeze in hoards of commuters and transport them to and fro from work.

Typical of a developing country, the black African population has a relatively large percentage of children under the age of fifteen years old – almost a third of the population. The camaraderie between these kids, on the streets and in their playgrounds, is tangible.

A sprawling sea of settlements. Imaginative names of these towns include Barcelona; Boys Town; Happy Valley; Bhambay; Tambo Square; Crossroads; Vietnam and Sweet Home.

A hot sweet mug of coffee on a chilly winter morning. A typical breakfast would also include hot mealie meal porridge – a staple product of South Africa.

An eclectic mix of pastels and brights, iron and cardboard, home

to these two brothers and siblings playing with a wire toy car.

A young boy enjoys a quiet moment in the setting sun on the doorstep of his home.

On the surface, these dwellings certainly have no remarkable architectural value, but beyond that, they are spiritual abodes, places of refuge, conversation, the warmth of kindred spirits.

While most homes have relied on paraffin lamps, oil or gas more and more have been blessed with the convenience of electricity. Power lines zigzag in a disorderly fashion, bringing the accessibility that most modern homes take for granted. Television, refrigeration, light, hot water and telephones.

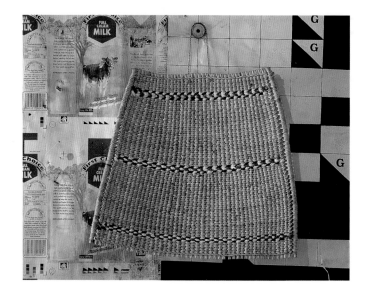

House-proud. With a shortage of money comes an abundance of ingenuity. Packaging over-runs have been used as wallpaper in a riot of pattern and colour. A straw bag becomes a decorative wall hanging. The rest of the country is sitting up and taking notice and some upmarket décor shops have emulated these fresh ideas.

It may seem incongruous, but street numbers identify the houses so that post may be delivered to their doors. Whether you're visiting a family home, or an international tourist resting at one of the growing numbers of B&B's in these colourful informal settlements, the doors will always open welcomingly.

Eric Miller / africanpictures.net

A dazzling washing detergent billboard. A boldness of blazing colour. The lustre of light-reflecting surfaces. Shanty towns are alive with an almost surreal illumination. But it is the beauty of the people that ultimately shines through.

On dry and derelict plains, in the ugly face of poverty, these individuals can still hold up their heads in dignity and pride. They've overcome arduous obstacles and turned everything around to show the world a rare and imaginative beauty – their homes, their shanty towns.

Jodi Bieber - South Photographs /africanpictures.net

PHOTOGRAPHERS

Gcinumuzi Ndwalane - *pg 6-7, 9-13, 24-25, 27, 32-35, 42, 44, 47, 53, 56-57, 59*

Neil Austen - *pg 1, 4, 16-17, 21, 31, 36-39, 43, 46, 48, 52, 58, 60-61*

John Hone - *pg 2, 22, 41*

Other contributions by:

Jodi Bieber - South Photographs /africanpictures.net - *pg 63, 64*

David Larsen - The Media Bank /africanpictures.net - *pg 14*

Cedric Nunn /africanpictures.net - *pg 18*

Eric Miller /africanpictures.net - *pg 50, 62*

Guy Stubbs /africanpictures.net - *pg 26, 28, 40, 54*

Produced by Art Publishers (Pty) Ltd

Durban, Johannesburg, Cape Town